D0849863

TO THE MILKY WAY AND
BEYOND
EXPLORATION OUTSIDE THE SOLAR SYSTEM

BY CHARLIE LIGHT

Gareth Stevens
PUBLISHING

Please visit our website, www.garethstevens.com. For a free color catalog of all our high-quality books, call toll free 1-800-542-2595 or fax 1-877-542-2596.

Library of Congress Cataloging-in-Publication Data

Names: Light, Charlie, author.
Title: To the Milky Way and beyond: exploration outside the solar system / Charlie Light.
Description: New York : Gareth Stevens Publishing, [2021] | Series:
   Liftoff! space exploration | Includes bibliographical references and
   index. | Contents: Home sweet home – Our place in the universe –
   Discovering the Milky Way – Understanding the Milky Way – A yardstick
   to the universe – Finding a neighbor – Spiral galaxies – Elliptical
   galaxies – Irregular galaxies – Exploring the Milky Way – The Hubble
   Space Telescope – Beyond the Milky Way.
Identifiers: LCCN 2020004047 | ISBN 9781538258842 (library binding) | ISBN
   9781538258828 (paperback) | ISBN 9781538258835 | ISBN 9781538258859
   (ebook)
Subjects: LCSH: Galaxies–Juvenile literature. | Milky Way–Juvenile
   literature.
Classification: LCC QB857.7 .L54 2021 | DDC 523.1/12–dc23
LC record available at https://lccn.loc.gov/2020004047

First Edition

Published in 2021 by
Gareth Stevens Publishing
111 East 14th Street, Suite 349
New York, NY 10003

Copyright © 2021 Gareth Stevens Publishing

Designer: Katelyn E. Reynolds
Editor: Abby Badach Doyle

Photo credits: Cover, p. 1 Alex Mit/Shutterstock.com; cover, pp. 1–32 (series background) David M. Schrader/Shutterstock.com; p. 5 Scott Cramer/ The Image Bank / Getty Images Plus; p. 7 Nasky/Shutterstock.com; p. 9 Universal History Archive/Getty Images; p. 11 elladoro/ iStock / Getty Images Plus; p. 12 Bettmann/Getty Images; pp. 13, 29 NASA; p. 15 courtesy of the Library of Congress; pp. 17, 19 NASA/JPL-Caltech; p. 21 NASA & ESA; p. 23 NASA Goddard; p. 25 Fabio Palmieri / EyeEm/Getty Images; p. 27 NASA , ESA , and the Hubble Heritage Team (STScI /AURA).

All rights reserved. No part of this book may be reproduced in any form without permission in writing from the publisher, except by a reviewer.

Printed in the United States of America

Some of the images in this book illustrate individuals who are models. The depictions do not imply actual situations or events.

CPSIA compliance information: Batch #CS20GS: For further information contact Gareth Stevens, New York, New York at 1-800-542-2595.

Find us on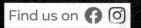

CONTENTS

Home Sweet Home..4

Our Place in the Universe.......................................6

Discovering the Milky Way.....................................8

Understanding the Milky Way...............................10

A Yardstick to the Universe..................................14

Finding a Neighbor..16

Spiral Galaxies...18

Elliptical Galaxies...20

Irregular Galaxies..22

Exploring the Milky Way.......................................24

The Hubble Space Telescope................................26

Beyond the Milky Way..28

Glossary...30

For More Information...31

Index..32

WORDS IN THE GLOSSARY APPEAR IN **BOLD** TYPE
THE FIRST TIME THEY ARE USED IN THE TEXT.

HOME SWEET HOME

You're reading this book on planet Earth, the third planet from the sun. It's the only one in our galaxy known to support life. Our galaxy is called the Milky Way. Like all galaxies, it's a large group of stars, planets, and dust that are pulled toward each other by the force of gravity.

It's hard to understand just how small our planet is compared to our massive galaxy. It's even harder to imagine how tiny our galaxy is compared to the universe! When you look up on a starry night, you're looking at the Milky Way. All the stars and planets that can be seen with the naked eye, or without a telescope, are part of the galaxy we call home.

INTERSTELLAR INFORMATION

ANCIENT GREEKS GAVE THE MILKY WAY ITS NAME. THEY CALLED IT "GALACTOS," WHICH MEANS "THE MILKY THING IN THE SKY." THE WORD "GALAXY" ALSO COMES FROM "GALACTOS."

HOW BIG IS THE MILKY WAY?

It's hard to know the exact number of stars in the Milky Way. Scientists believe it has more than 100 billion stars. We measure our galaxy's diameter in light-years. A light-year is just what it sounds like. It's a unit of distance measurement based on how far light travels in a year. Diameter is a measurement from one side of an object to the other. This measurement passes through the center point. One light-year is about 6 trillion miles (9 trillion km). Our galaxy is about 100,000 light-years wide in diameter.

OUR PLACE
IN THE UNIVERSE

Humans have a history of believing we're the center of everything. Early **astronomers** thought Earth was the center of the universe. They thought Earth didn't move and that the sun, stars, and planets orbited us. This idea is called the geocentric model of the universe. A model is a small version of a bigger thing.

Astronomers started finding problems with the geocentric model in the 900s CE. It was discovered that Earth is rotating, or turning. That's why the sun and stars seem to move across the sky. Iranian **philosopher** Abu Rayhan Biruni thought Earth orbited the sun. Both of these things are true! Polish astronomer Nicolaus Copernicus built on these ideas in the 1500s. His work is called the heliocentric model.

INTERSTELLAR INFORMATION

THE WORD "GEOCENTRIC" MEANS EARTH-CENTERED. "HELIOCENTRIC" MEANS SUN-CENTERED. BOTH MODELS ARE NAMED AFTER THE OBJECT AT THE CENTER.

GEOCENTRIC

HELIOCENTRIC

ONE OF THE EARLIEST WRITTEN ACCOUNTS OF THE GEOCENTRIC MODEL WAS BY PTOLEMY, AN EGYPTIAN ASTRONOMER BORN AROUND 100 CE. PEOPLE BELIEVED THIS FOR YEARS UNTIL THE HELIOCENTRIC MODEL WAS DISCOVERED.

RELIGION AND SCIENCE

The geocentric model was a big part of many religious beliefs. This was especially true for Christianity. It became part of the Catholic Church's beliefs in the Middle Ages. The Church saw Earth as their God's most important creation. It saw outer space as heavens. These are places with religious meaning for Catholics. Heliocentrism went against the Catholic Church's beliefs. Ideas that go against a religion are called heresy. The Catholic Church banned Copernicus' writing.

DISCOVERING THE MILKY WAY

The more humans learned about space, the smaller Earth seemed. In the late 1500s, Italian philosopher Giordano Bruno wrote that the universe was infinite, or never-ending. He thought Earth was just one of an infinite number of worlds. We had to learn more about outer space to find out if this was true. Was the universe infinite, or did it have an end?

Our next leap forward was understanding the Milky Way. To the human eye, it just looks like milky clouds. Cloudy parts of space are called nebulae. Italian astronomer Galileo Galilei was the first person to see the Milky Way clearly. He looked at it through a telescope in 1610. He saw that the "clouds" were actually stars grouped together.

INTERSTELLAR INFORMATION

LONG BEFORE TELESCOPES, THE GREEK PHILOSOPHER DEMOCRITUS GUESSED THE MILKY WAY'S "CLOUDS" WERE MADE UP OF STARS. HE WAS RIGHT!

THE CATHOLIC CHURCH DIDN'T ADMIT GALILEO GALILEI WAS CORRECT UNTIL 1992. THE CHURCH APOLOGIZED FOR GALILEI'S **TRIAL** 359 YEARS AFTER HIS DEATH.

GALILEO

THE ROMAN INQUISITION

It took a long time for people to believe that Earth wasn't the center of the universe. The Catholic Church called this idea heresy, and heresy was a crime. This crime was punished by part of the Church called the Inquisition. Giordano Bruno was killed by the Roman Inquisition for his ideas in 1600. The Roman Inquisition also placed Galileo Galilei under house arrest for believing in heliocentrism. He couldn't leave for the rest of his life.

UNDERSTANDING THE MILKY WAY

It took a long time for humans to understand how big the universe is. For a long time, most astronomers thought the Milky Way was the only galaxy. English astronomer Thomas Wright was ahead of his time. In 1750, Wright wrote that the Milky Way was a layer of stars. This layer was shaped like a disk, and these stars were held together by gravity. The Milky Way was like our solar system, but much bigger! He realized that our solar system was part of the Milky Way.

Wright thought that there were other galaxies too. He thought nebulae might be galaxies outside our own. Today we know nebulae are giant clouds of gas and dust in space. They form when stars are created or weaken. To understand more about nebulae, humans first had to learn more about the Milky Way.

INTERSTELLAR INFORMATION

GERMAN PHILOSOPHER IMMANUEL KANT ALSO THOUGHT NEBULAE WERE OUTSIDE THE MILKY WAY. HE CALLED THESE NEBULAE "ISLAND UNIVERSES." HE THOUGHT THEY WERE ENTIRE UNIVERSES OUTSIDE OUR OWN!

OTHER GALAXIES

Today, we know that humans can see three other galaxies without telescopes. These are the Large Magellanic Cloud, the Small Magellanic Cloud, and the Andromeda Galaxy. The Magellanic Clouds are our closest neighbors. The Andromeda Galaxy is 2.5 million light-years away! It looks like a fuzzy star to the human eye. Persian astronomer Abd al-Rahman al-Sufi was the first person to observe other galaxies. He wrote about the Andromeda Galaxy and the Large Magellanic Cloud galaxy.

11

William Herschel studied stars in the late 1700s. He found that one part of the sky had a larger number of stars. This was the Milky Way's core, or center. Herschel thought that our solar system was part of the Milky Way's core. This later turned out to be wrong.

Harlow Shapley was an astronomer in the early 1900s. He worked at the Mount Wilson Observatory in California. At the time, this observatory had the biggest telescope in the world. Shapley found that our solar system is far from the center of the Milky Way. We are out on the fringe, or a far end of the Milky Way.

INTERSTELLAR INFORMATION

HARLOW SHAPLEY STUDIED SPHERE-SHAPED GROUPS OF STARS. THESE ARE CALLED GLOBULAR CLUSTERS. HE FOUND MOST OF THE 150 GLOBULAR CLUSTERS IN THE MILKY WAY.

◄ HARLOW SHAPLEY

THE BIG DEBATE ABOUT NEBULAE

During Shapley's time, we still weren't sure if nebulae were part of our galaxy or not. Shapley thought these cloudy parts of space were part of the Milky Way. He thought we were the only galaxy in the universe. Astronomer Heber Curtis disagreed. He thought these nebulae were other galaxies far away. The two astronomers had a **debate** about nebulae in 1920. This debate still didn't answer the question, though!

13

A YARDSTICK
TO THE UNIVERSE

American astronomer Henrietta Leavitt worked at the Harvard College Observatory in Cambridge, Massachusetts. She volunteered at first, and then joined the full-time staff in 1902. She studied Cepheid stars, which go through a cycle of dimming and brightening. Leavitt found that the brighter a Cepheid star could shine, the longer it would shine brightly. This made it possible to figure out a Cepheid star's magnitude. A star's magnitude is its highest level of brightness.

Leavitt knew she could use a star's magnitude to figure out how far away it was. She used math equations to do this. She published her research in 1912. Her math made it possible to measure up to 10 million light-years! Before her math, we could only measure about 100 light-years at a time.

INTERSTELLAR INFORMATION

LEAVITT'S MATH BECAME KNOWN AS "THE YARDSTICK TO THE UNIVERSE." IT LET US MEASURE FARTHER THAN EVER BEFORE.

THROUGHOUT HER LIFETIME, HENRIETTA LEAVITT
DISCOVERED 2,400 CEPHEID STARS.

MEASURING THE MILKY WAY

Shapley used Henrietta Leavitt's math to measure the diameter of the Milky Way. He found that the Milky Way was about 300,000 light-years in diameter. He also thought our sun was 50,000 light-years away from the Milky Way's center. Shapley's measurements were pretty close! Today, our measurements show us that the Milky Way is about 100,000 light-years in diameter and the sun is roughly 30,000 light-years away from the center.

15

FINDING
A NEIGHBOR

Henrietta Leavitt's work made other discoveries possible. She helped answer the big questions about nebulae: Were they part of the Milky Way, or were there other galaxies?

American astronomer Edwin Hubble believed nebulae were outside the Milky Way. He took photos of a Cepheid star from a nebula over time. He noticed that its brightness changed over about 31 days. Then, he used Leavitt's math to find the Cepheid's magnitude. That helped him find out how far away the Cepheid was from Earth. It was about 900,000 light-years away. The Milky Way was only 100,000 light-years across. This meant the Cepheid star—and the nebula—were outside the Milky Way! This nebula is now called the Andromeda Galaxy. It proved our galaxy isn't the only one in the universe.

INTERSTELLAR INFORMATION

THE ANDROMEDA GALAXY AND THE MILKY WAY ARE MOVING TOWARDS EACH OTHER! IN ABOUT 4 BILLION YEARS, THE TWO GALAXIES WILL COLLIDE. THIS MEANS THEY WILL "HIT" EACH OTHER.

THE ANDROMEDA GALAXY IS ALSO
KNOWN AS MESSIER 31, OR M31.

CEPHEID STARS

Astronomers later discovered there are two kinds of Cepheid stars—Population I and Population II. Population I Cepheids are younger and brighter. They're better for measuring distance. During Leavitt's time, astronomers thought all Cepheids worked like Population I stars. Population II Cepheids are older and dimmer. The Cepheid in the Andromeda Galaxy that Edwin Hubble studied was actually a Population II Cepheid. The math for these works a little differently.

SPIRAL GALAXIES

Once scientists realized there are galaxies outside our own, they needed a way to sort them. Astronomers label galaxies by their shape. There are three main shapes: spiral, elliptical, and irregular. Spiral galaxies look like flat disks. They have a center that bulges out. The center has a large number of stars. Arms curve around the center, giving the galaxy its spiral shape. The arms are made of young stars, gas, and dust.

Spiral galaxies are surrounded by a circle of stars. This circle is called a halo. The galaxy's older stars are in the center and halo. Some spiral galaxies have a long center that's stretched out like a bar. These are called barred spiral galaxies. The Milky Way is a barred spiral galaxy.

INTERSTELLAR INFORMATION

ASTRONOMERS AREN'T SURE WHY THE MILKY WAY IS TWISTED. IT MIGHT HAVE BECOME TWISTED BY COMBINING WITH SMALLER GALAXIES IN THE PAST. THE GRAVITY IN ITS ARMS MIGHT BE PULLING IT INTO A TWISTED SHAPE.

THIS ARTIST'S VIEW OF THE MILKY WAY SHOWS ITS TWO MAJOR AND TWO MINOR ARMS. IT IS BASED ON IMAGES TAKEN FROM THE SPITZER SPACE TELESCOPE.

HOW OUR GALAXY IS LIKE A POTATO CHIP

In 2019, astronomers learned that the Milky Way is not a flat disk. It's actually curved, like a potato chip! A new map shows how our galaxy looks like a potato chip that's been twisted. It's hard to see the bend looking up from where we are on Earth. Astronomers found this new information about the Milky Way's shape by studying Cepheid stars. Henrietta Leavitt's math is still helping us understand our galaxy and beyond today!

ELLIPTICAL GALAXIES

Elliptical galaxies have an oval shape, like a circle that has been stretched out. They have less dust and gas than spiral galaxies. Their stars are spread out evenly. They're often made of older, dimmer stars. Astronomers think **black holes** might stop new stars from forming in elliptical galaxies.

Elliptical galaxies are the most common type of galaxy in the universe. They're made when galaxies collide. The individual galaxies lose their shape, becoming one big elliptical galaxy. When another galaxy collides with an elliptical galaxy, they can form a very strange new galaxy. This is how the Sombrero Galaxy formed. This is an elliptical galaxy with a disk-shaped galaxy inside it. It looks like a kind of hat called a sombrero.

INTERSTELLAR INFORMATION

ONE OF THE LARGEST GALAXIES IN THE UNIVERSE IS AN ELLIPTICAL GALAXY CALLED M87. IT HAS TRILLIONS OF STARS! CHARLES MESSIER DISCOVERED M87 IN 1781.

TYPES OF GALAXIES

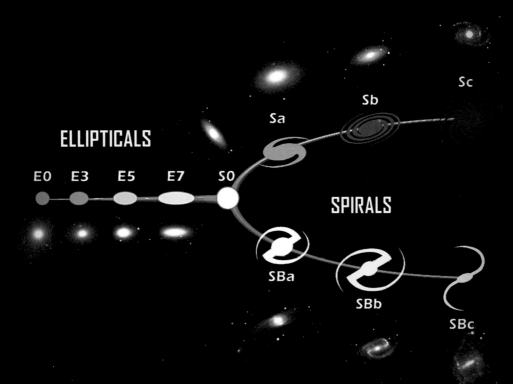

ELLIPTICALS

E0   E3   E5   E7   S0

Sa

Sb

Sc

SPIRALS

SBa

SBb

SBc

THIS IS HUBBLE'S TUNING FORK, WHICH ORGANIZES GALAXIES. THE GALAXIES THAT BEGIN WITH "E" ARE ELLIPTICALS. THE "S0" GALAXY STANDS FOR LENTICULAR GALAXIES. THE GALAXIES THAT BEGIN WITH "S" ARE SPIRALS.

THE HUBBLE TUNING FORK

Edwin Hubble classified, or sorted, galaxies by shape. He drew a diagram of his classes of galaxies. This diagram is called "Hubble's tuning fork" because of its shape. It looks like a musical tool called a tuning fork. Hubble sorted galaxies into ellipticals and spirals. Each group was broken into specific types. Hubble also found some galaxies that were in between ellipticals and spirals. He called these lenticular galaxies. Astronomers still use Hubble's classes today.

IRREGULAR GALAXIES

Some galaxies don't have a clear elliptical or spiral shape. These are called irregular galaxies. They come in all sorts of shapes. Some look like they used to be elliptical or spiral galaxies. They may have a bar of stars through their center. Others have no clear shape at all. Irregular galaxies are generally smaller and younger. They're often very bright because their stars are so young. Many irregular galaxies have lots of dust and gas.

Our closest neighbors—the Magellanic Clouds—are irregular galaxies. These two galaxies have bars of stars in their centers. They formed about 13 billion years ago. That's around when our galaxy formed too! The Magellanic Clouds orbit the Milky Way. For that reason, they are called **satellite** galaxies.

INTERSTELLAR INFORMATION

THE BIGGEST, BRIGHTEST STAR HUMANS HAVE FOUND IS IN THE LARGE MAGELLANIC CLOUD. IT'S CALLED R136A1. IT'S MORE THAN 300 TIMES AS MASSIVE AS OUR SUN!

THIS PHOTO FROM THE HUBBLE SPACE TELESCOPE SHOWS BRIGHT NEBULAE IN THE LARGE MAGELLANIC CLOUD. THIS IS A SIGN OF NEW STARS BEING BORN!

OUR GALACTIC NEIGHBORHOOD

Scientists put the Milky Way in a collection of about 30 other galaxies. This group, called the Local Group, is spread out over 10 million light-years. Edwin Hubble was the first person to recognize the Local Group. Our galaxy is near the middle of the group. The Milky Way and the Andromeda Galaxy are the two most massive galaxies in the Local Group. Astronomers think the Local Group could collide with another group of galaxies called the Virgo Cluster.

EXPLORING
THE MILKY WAY

    The Milky Way has two major arms and two minor arms. Our solar system is two-thirds of the way down one of the smaller ones. Earth shares the solar system with seven other planets. There are thousands of other planets in the Milky Way. They're outside our solar system, orbiting other stars. These are called exoplanets.

    We've only explored a tiny bit of our own solar system. Humans have done most space exploration with satellites, unmanned spacecraft, and robots. Earth's moon is the only surface besides Earth that humans have visited! Only 12 people have walked on the moon. They were all from the United States' space program, the National **Aeronautics** and Space Administration (NASA). Russia, Japan, China, the European Space Agency, and India have all sent **probes** to the moon.

INTERSTELLAR INFORMATION

AMERICAN ASTRONAUTS NEIL ARMSTRONG AND EDWIN "BUZZ" ALDRIN BECAME THE FIRST HUMANS TO WALK ON THE MOON IN 1969. THEY WERE PART OF THE *APOLLO II* MISSION, ALONG WITH MICHAEL COLLINS.

THERE'S STILL SO MUCH TO EXPLORE IN THE MILKY WAY. ON AVERAGE, EACH STAR YOU CAN SEE IN THE NIGHT SKY HAS AT LEAST ONE PLANET ORBITING IT.

MARS EXPLORATION

Mars and Venus are the two planets closest to Earth. Scientists discovered that Mars likely had water on its surface many years ago. This made scientists wonder if there was ever life on Mars. There have been more missions to Mars than any other planet in the solar system. NASA has explored Mars using rovers. These are robots with wheels that can move over difficult ground. NASA is also planning to send humans to Mars someday.

THE HUBBLE SPACE TELESCOPE

Humans have explored our galaxy right from Earth using telescopes. However, Earth's atmosphere blocked the light from galaxies far away. Even though we built better telescopes, the atmosphere still limited how much we could see. In 1923, German scientist Hermann Oberth had the idea to send a telescope into space. This would allow humans to get a clearer view of our galactic neighborhood.

In 1990, the European Space Agency and NASA sent the first telescope to space. It was first called the Large Space Telescope, but was renamed the Hubble Space Telescope (HST) in honor of astronomer Edwin Hubble. The HST was sent into space with a flaw that made its pictures blurry. Three years later, NASA sent a mission to fix the HST. It started taking clear photos in 1993.

INTERSTELLAR INFORMATION

THE HST HAS DISCOVERED INCREDIBLE THINGS. ONE OF THE MOST EXCITING IS POSSIBLE PROOF OF WATER ON EUROPA, ONE OF JUPITER'S MOONS. THIS COULD ALSO BE A SIGN OF LIFE!

THE HST TOOK A FAMOUS PHOTO, CALLED THE PILLARS OF CREATION, IN 1995. IT SHOWS STAR-FORMING REGIONS IN THE EAGLE NEBULA. THE HST RE-TOOK THE PHOTO IN HIGHER DEFINITION IN 2014.

TELESCOPE TIME MACHINE

The HST let humans see farther than ever before, but we're still looking into the past. Light takes time to travel. We see light as it looked when it began traveling, not what it looks like in the present. The Andromeda Galaxy is 2.5 million light-years away from Earth. That means we're seeing what it looked like 2.5 million years ago. The HST has taken photos of the Magellanic Clouds and the Andromeda Galaxy.

BEYOND
THE MILKY WAY

In the 1920s, research showed that the farther away a galaxy was from Earth, the faster it was moving away from us. This is known as the Hubble-Lemaître law, after Edwin Hubble and Belgian scientist Georges Lemaître. This law means that the whole universe is expanding, or stretching!

Lemaître came up with the idea that the universe began with one atom. This atom held all the matter in the universe. It expanded over 13.8 billion years—and is still expanding today. This idea became known as the big bang **theory**. Today, astronomers have found that the universe is expanding even faster. Our galactic neighbors are moving farther away. Someday, they could move away from us faster than the speed of light.

INTERSTELLAR INFORMATION

NO ONE IS SURE IF OR HOW THE UNIVERSE WILL END. ONE IDEA IS THAT IT WILL CONTRACT, OR SHRINK BACK INTO ITSELF. THIS THEORY IS CALLED THE BIG CRUNCH.

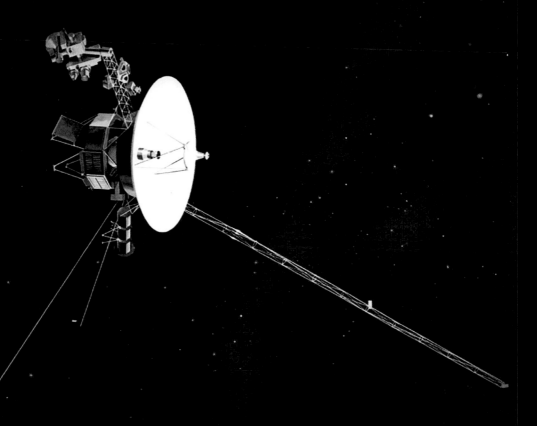

NASA'S VOYAGER I PROBE HAS GONE FARTHER AWAY FROM EARTH THAN ANY HUMAN-MADE OBJECT. IT REACHED INTERSTELLAR SPACE IN 2012. "INTERSTELLAR" MEANS THE SPACE BETWEEN STARS.

ARE THERE OTHER UNIVERSES?

Some scientists believe there are many universes—not just one. This idea is called the multiverse theory. There are many different ideas about how these other universes might have formed. Humans have come up with theories that explain basic things about how our universe works, such as gravity and motion. These theories are called laws. If other universes exist, they might have completely different laws than ours. We might discover more someday. . .or we may never know!

GLOSSARY

aeronautics: a science that deals with airplanes and flying

astronomer: a person who studies stars, planets, and other heavenly bodies

black hole: an invisible part of space with so much gravity that light can't escape it

debate: an argument or public discussion

philosopher: a person who tries to discover and to understand the nature of knowledge

probe: an unmanned spaceship

theory: an explanation based on facts that is generally accepted by scientists

trial: a formal meeting to determine someone's guilt or innocence

satellite: an object that circles Earth. Also, an object that circles Earth in order to collect and send information or aid in communication.

FOR MORE INFORMATION

BOOKS

Betts, Bruce. *Super Cool Space Facts: A Fun, Fact-Filled Space Book for Kids.* Berkeley, CA: Rockridge Press, 2019.

Outer Space. Bath, England: Parragon Books, 2015.

Space!: The Universe as You've Never Seen It Before. New York, NY: DK Children, 2015.

WEBSITES

ESA Kids
www.esa.int/kids/en/learn/Our_Universe/Stars_and_galaxies/The_Milky_Way
Explore the Milky Way at the European Space Agency's site for kids.

NASA Kids' Club
www.nasa.gov/kidsclub/index.html
Learn more about the Milky Way and beyond at NASA's site for kids.

Planets for Kids
www.planetsforkids.org/galaxies/milky-way.html
Dive into outer space at this fun site.

Publisher's note to educators and parents: Our editors have carefully reviewed these websites to ensure that they are suitable for students. Many websites change frequently, however, and we cannot guarantee that a site's future contents will continue to meet our high standards of quality and educational value. Be advised that students should be closely supervised whenever they access the internet.

INDEX

Andromeda Galaxy 11, 16, 17, 23, 27

big bang theory 28

big crunch 28

black hole 20

Bruno, Giordano 8, 9

Cepheid stars 14, 15, 16, 17, 19

Copernicus, Nicolaus 6, 7

elliptical galaxy 18, 20, 21, 22

geocentric model 6, 7

globular cluster 12, 13

heliocentric model 6, 7

Herschel, William 12

Hubble Space Telescope (HST) 26, 27

irregular galaxy 18, 22

Large Magellanic Clouds 11, 22, 23

Leavitt, Henrietta 14, 15, 16, 17, 19

Mars 25

Mount Wilson Observatory 12

National Aeronautics and Space Administration (NASA) 24, 25, 26, 29

nebulae 8, 10, 13, 16, 23, 27

probes 24, 29

Small Magellanic Clouds 11

spiral galaxy 18, 20, 21, 22

Venus 25

Wright, Thomas 10